Supply Chain Management, Inventory Control, Human Resource Management, and Customer Service

Louis Bevoc

Published by
NutriNiche System LLC

Louis Bevoc books...simple explanations of complex subjects

Supply Chain Management in Manufacturing
A Basic Introduction

Louis Bevoc

Published by
NutriNiche System LLC

Louis Bevoc books...simple explanations of complex subjects

Introduction 5
Components 5
    Strategical 6
    Tactical 6
    Operational 6
Goals and objectives 7
    Fill customer orders 7
    Improve customer service 8
    Add customer value 8
    Embrace change 8
    Manage risks 8
    Add stakeholder value 9
    Utilize resources 9
    Establish trust 9
    Promote financial success
Advantages 9
    Quality 9
    Inventory 10
    Purchasing 10
    Production 11
    Distribution 11
    Cost 12
    Teamwork 12
    Risk 13
Disadvantages 13
    Complexity 13
    Time 14
    Trust 14
    Foreign laws 14
    Uncertainty 14
Improving 15
    Involve employees 15
    Improve technology 15
    Encourage innovation 15
    Utilize information 15

Review performance 16
Analyze returns 16
Summary 16

Introduction

A book on supply chain management in manufacturing (SCM) would not be complete without a discussion on purchasing because manufacturers need to purchase raw materials and supplies to produce finished products. Not surprisingly, those raw materials and supplies do not magically show up at the doorstep…they have to be ordered by purchasing agents in a timely fashion at the best possible price.

Purchasing agents, also known as buyers, follow designated company strategies when making buying decisions. They often adhere to a just-in-time philosophy where raw materials and supplies are brought in only when needed. Excessive inventory needs to be avoided due to the money that gets tied up, and all decisions are made with cost in mind.

In the past, purchasing for manufacturers was primarily done by lower-level employees. A manager told a clerical worker what was needed, and the order was placed. However, strategic purchasing has made this process a relic of the past that will likely never return. Purchasing is now done by management personnel who have a great deal of authority and responsibility, and it is a major part of supply chain management…the focus of this book.

Supply chain management is a controlled system where organizations along the entire supply chain work together to produce and deliver the best possible products at the lowest cost. Shared resources are used to assure purchasing, production, and distribution are effective and efficient while meeting established quality standards. This gives producers of products a competitive advantage in today's lean manufacturing environment.

In the global marketplace, many manufacturers rely on outsourcing and suppliers to do some of their production. This works well for getting products made, but reliance on others brings about quality concerns. Those concerns are the reason that the modern era of supply chain management came into play.

Now that you have a basic understanding of the relationship between supply chain management and manufacturing, let's move on to the basic components involved with this association.

Components

In manufacturing, SCM manages the flow of goods from the purchasing of raw materials to the delivery of finished products…including the storage and inventorying of all stock. The plan is to synchronize supply and demand while monitoring and controlling all activities along the chain. Based on this plan, it is rather obvious that good communication is critical at all levels.

SCM utilizes logistics, engineering, operations, and technology to accomplish manufacturing goals and objectives. For example, inventory levels of raw materials and finished products must always be accessible for reordering, production scheduling, and fulfillment of customer orders. Modern bar coding technology has made this possible because it has the ability to receive information about inventory that includes past and present location, quantities, and future destination.

Essentially, supply chain management in manufacturing can be broken down into three major phases as follows:

Strategical

This is the planning stage. A road map for the SCM needs to be developed, and supply chain partners need to be identified. Where, when, and how will the finished products be manufactured? Who will supply the raw materials? Is another company going to manufacture part or all of the finished products? Where will the finished products be warehoused? These questions need to be answered during the strategical phase, and those answers are best achieved using collaboration from all partners in the chain. For example, companies need input from each other to figure out what makes the most sense from a logistical standpoint and which organization is most capable of manufacturing specific products.

Tactical

This is the execution stage. It involves putting the plan into effect and finalizing the details. What quantity of raw materials and finished products will be inventoried? What are the costs associated with raw materials and finished products? What are the quality specifications for raw materials and finished products? These questions need to be answered during the tactical phase, and those answers are best achieved using collaboration from all partners in the chain. For example, it might seem like the quality specifications should be set by the manufacturers, but they need input from their suppliers for realistic expectations. Along the same lines, suppliers need to communicate with manufacturers about costs so the best economical solutions can be obtained.

Operational

This is the maintenance stage. It is where the day-to-day activities are managed to ensure the supply chain runs efficiently and effectively. It entails all plant activities including purchasing, receiving, production, inventory, storage, and shipping. What types of raw materials need to be ordered? What types of raw materials need to be inventoried? What types of finished products need to be manufactured? What types of finished products need to be inventoried? These questions need to be answered during the operational phase, and those answers are best achieved using collaboration from all partners in the chain. For example, manufacturers need distributors to help them make production decisions, and they need to communicate with suppliers about fulfilling raw material needs.

The above phases are necessary components of effective supply chain management for manufacturers. However, other factors also influence SCM. These factors include environmental concerns and ethical responsibilities.

In terms of the environment, production facilities are capable of creating a wealth of pollution. This pollution can contaminate the ground, water, and air…and none of it is acceptable. This concern for the environment is not new for manufacturers, but SCM raises the bar because every organization in the chain must be environmentally responsible.

Ethical responsibilities also affect SCM. Ethics are a serious issue for manufacturers that employ low-paid production workers...especially if those manufacturers compete globally. There is a worldwide concern for how employees are treated, and organizations that are perceived as abusing their workers face backlash. Repercussions might be limited to verbal criticism, but they can also be much more severe....including the boycotting of products. Reduced sales can injure organizations and even put them out of business, so ethical issues do need to be addressed. Similar to environmental concerns, ethical responsibilities affect the entire supply chain.

Now you understand the major phases of supply chain management and some additional factors that affect the process. However, these components do not explain why this process is implemented by so many organizations. This leads us to the next section that discusses the goals and objectives manufacturers have in mind when they implement SCM.

Goals and objectives

Supply chain management is, to say the least, a complex arrangement. Every organization in the chain must be successful for it to be effective. Money, time, and human resources are required to establish relationships, define roles, implement new technology, and bring everything together for a smooth flowing system.

Sometimes the amount of work required to obtain successful SCM does not seem worth it. However, once the system is running, the benefits convince most people that their efforts were not in vain. In fact, those efforts usually pay off tenfold when goals and objectives are achieved. This raises a question. What exactly are the goals of supply chain management? The following lists SCM goals and describes their relationship to manufacturing:

Fill customer orders

This is the most basic goal of supply chain management. If finished products are not in stock, then customer orders will not be filled. The entire supply chain must work together to achieve this objective, and a week or broken link can cause a breakdown that leads to failure. Fortunately, most organizations make order fulfillment a top priority, and they tend to do whatever is necessary to achieve this objective. For example, management at a furniture manufacturer understands that a customer with a chain of retail office supply stores puts leather desk chairs on sale every June for the entire month. Based on this, they make sure they have 1000 leather desk chairs in stock at the beginning of March every year so they can fill the orders they receive.

Improve customer service

Order fulfillment is only a portion of good customer service. The other part involves meeting customer needs and expectations. In addition to filling orders, customers also want products delivered on time to specified receiving points. In other words, manufacturers must be able to ship products in a timely manner to any location, or customer expectations will not be met. For example, a dental manufacturing company that produces cavity filling compounds has a customer with 35 mobile dental labs that travel around the nation to perform low-cost dentistry on people who do not have dental insurance. This manufacturer knows they must have the compound in stock and be able to ship anywhere in the nation, so they have worked out a deal with UPS to pick up products every day at their facility for overnight delivery. This assures products will be delivered on time anywhere in the country.

Add customer value

Filling customer orders and improving customer service are both important objectives for supply chain management, but manufacturers also have to keep in mind the need to create value for their customers. Value is created by understanding and exceeding the requirements that makeup customer service. For example, management at an automotive supplier understands that their customers regard just-in-time (JIT) delivery as a top priority. Rather than scheduling deliveries with the lowest-cost carriers on a case-by-case basis, the supplier enters into an agreement with a specific carrier that makes sure delivery trucks are available 24/7. This creates value by assuring customers that they will receive the parts they need at the times they want them.

Embrace change

Change can be difficult because it often requires people to leave their comfort zones. They have to enter unfamiliar areas causing them to fear the unknown. A major goal of SCM is to help manufacturers embrace change as they modify and adjust their behavior in different situations. Confidence is the key here, and that confidence is based on the fact that a variety of expertise is readily available with a simple email or phone call. At some point, change is going to happen to all manufacturers...so they might as well accept and embrace it for an easier transition.

Manage risks

At first glance, this might seem a bit strange. After all, why would managing risks be a goal of SCM? The answer lies in surviving workplace disruption. Over time, supply chains undergo changes...and some of those changes are catastrophic if they are not properly managed. Natural disasters, power failures, security problems, labor issues, and leadership changes are all events that can damage the flow of products and risk the survival of organizations. Risk management helps manufacturers identify, rectify, and move past disruption so they can redesign the supply chain and prevent future reoccurrences. Based on this, it makes sense that risk management is a goal of supply chain management.

Add stakeholder value

Stakeholders are people or organizations who are affected by a manufacturer's actions. This includes co-producers, suppliers, investors, communities, and government agencies. Value, similar to customer value, is created by understanding and exceeding stakeholder requirements. However, it differs from customer value because it can be driven by social requirements that are not necessarily financially beneficial to the manufacturer. For example, management at a meat processor understands the community they manufacture their products in wants a clean environment. Rather than monitoring the air quality for the smoke exhaust that exits their smokehouses, they install "scrubbers" on the exhaust stacks to reduce the amount of smoke that enters the atmosphere. This creates value by assuring the community that the air they breathe will not be polluted or contaminated.

Utilize resources

There are many different skills associated with supply chain management. Some organizations in the chain are great at production, others excel at inventory control, and still, others are highly efficient at warehousing and distribution. Every organization has specialization and expertise that helps them identify the best methods for completing job-related tasks while incorporating cutting-edge technology. A goal of manufacturers is to tap into this expertise and use it for a competitive advantage.

Establish trust

For manufacturers to achieve a competitive advantage, organizations on the supply chain need to trust each other. This means trusting that information will be accurate, costs will be shared, and responsibilities will be fulfilled. Mutual trust benefits every organization in the supply chain, and this is why it is a goal. Unfortunately, this goal can be the most difficult to obtain because once trust is lost, it is difficult to regain.

Promote financial success

This is likely the most well-known and important goal. Supply chain management needs to increase profitability or it is not operating as intended. Manufacturers strive to reduce inventory, labor, and freight costs while increasing order accuracy, investor return-on-investment, and customer satisfaction. This leads to more efficient operations...and greater financial success. The major reason that most manufacturers are in business is to make money, and supply chain management helps them accomplish this objective.

Now that you are aware of the major goals of supply chain management, let's move on to the advantages that occur after these goals are achieved.

Advantages

If supply chain management did not have advantages, it would not be used by manufacturers. Fortunately, the advantages are plentiful, thereby making this process very attractive. The following are specific areas where SCM is beneficial for manufacturing organizations:

Quality

This advantage of SCM has far-reaching effects. The quality associated with the items produced by manufacturers is one of the most important reasons those items are purchased, and that quality has been questionable over the past decade due to the changes made in many different industries. For example, some U.S.-based manufacturers have exported their production to India or China to reduce costs. This makes sense financially, but it presents challenges from a quality standpoint...and SCM incorporates techniques that help overcome those challenges. Standards such as those set by ISO (The International Organization for Standardization) can be used to make products more consistent, thereby increasing finished product quality. Compliance with these standards assures customers that products meet established criteria and eliminates the need for an overabundance of quality checks during the production process. In terms of quality, supply chain management creates a win-win situation for manufacturers and their customers.

Inventory

Inventory ties up valuable resources, and this is why many manufacturers strive to keep it minimal. Supply chain management reduces money and space requirements while providing the versatility needed to accurately fill customer orders. It does this by keeping inventory at established levels based on historical data and other information provided by the chain. The success experienced is a direct result of communication between organizations involved in the process. For example, suppliers monitor raw materials and deliver only when needed, thereby creating a JIT system inventory for production. At the other end of the chain, distributors keep manufacturers abreast of sales projections and trends. This reduces worry for manufacturing buyers and salespeople, thereby allowing them to focus on other important aspects of their jobs.

Purchasing

For some manufacturers, this is the biggest advantage because substantial amounts of money and space can be saved. To get a better understanding of why this is the case, the role of purchasing agents (also known as buyers) needs to be described.

Purchasing agents are involved in many important aspects of plant operations, but their main job responsibilities are replenishing the stock of existing materials and obtaining stock of new materials. This might sound fairly easy, but it is not. Many skills are required to be a top-notch buyer, and those skills typically come from experience. These skills include:

Negotiation

Buyers need the ability to work with others and create advantageous situations for the manufacturers that employ them. These advantages include payment terms, specifications, price, and guarantees. Guarantees can encompass delivery schedules, inventory quantities, product quality, and additional services provided by the vendor.

Management

Purchasing agents in manufacturing plants have a lot to manage. They need to oversee lead times, deliveries, pricing errors, and inventory levels. They also need to manage suppliers by providing them with information about changes and new requirements. In terms of management, buyers need to be astute...or they will likely let some aspects of their jobs get out of control.

Strategy

>This refers to the strategy of the manufacturer rather than that of the individual purchasing agent. Management sets goals, and buyers help accomplish those goals. They monitor inventory levels, look for product losses, watch for pricing changes, and keep an eye on developing trends. Their actions affect the direction of the manufacturers that employ them, and sometimes they are the single biggest factor involved in management strategy.

Price

>This is the most well-known skill required for purchasing agents. Buyers must be able to find the lowest price possible for the products or materials that best suit the manufacturer's needs. This should not be confused with simply finding the lowest price. There also needs to be value...and value is not always found in the cheapest commodity.
>
>Essentially, price skills accomplish two objectives. They (1) improve profits and (2) make manufacturers more competitive. Profitability makes shareholders happy, and competitiveness keeps businesses operating. In short, pricing is an important skill for buyers because it directly affects the survival of manufacturing organizations.

Awareness

>One might question why awareness is a skill. The answer is because, similar to a mother, a buyer's work is never done. There is a constant need to be vigilant about what is happening around them. This vigilance includes monitoring regulations, problems, policies, procedures, and changes...and reacting appropriately. As might be expected, this monitoring can never be taken lightheartedly or put to rest...and that is why awareness is an important skill of purchasing agents.

Production

Supply chain management works wonders in terms of improving production because innovation and technology lower labor costs while improving output. In SCM, every organization does what they do best and their combined efforts result in improved efficiency of the manufacturing process. Add this to the fact that organizations within the chain co-manufacture products in their areas of expertise, and the resulting production improvement becomes quite transparent. Since production is the heart of manufacturing, this advantage is one of the most important.

Distribution

It is difficult for manufacturers to be good at everything. They need to focus on getting products made that their customers need, and this means other aspects of the beginning-to-end process get less attention. Distribution is often one of those aspects, but it is not a problem with SCM because there are organizations in the chain that are logistical specialists. They make sure products get delivered to the customers that ordered them, and this relieves manufacturers of distribution-related responsibilities.

Cost

The importance of cost is typically a top concern for most manufacturers. When supply chains are properly managed, there are cost savings for everyone involved. This is because each organization does its part to reduce the work required for others, thereby making the overall process more efficient. For manufacturing organizations, this maximizes efficiency from the purchasing of raw materials to the delivery of finished goods…and it results in lower costs.

Teamwork

There is little doubt that teamwork is an advantage of SCM. People work together chain-wide to make manufacturers more efficient and competitive. Below are some benefits of teamwork as they relate to manufacturing:

Synergy

This might be the biggest advantage of teams because every member of the chain can exchange thoughts and entertain other perspectives. Each organization has unique strengths that add diversity to the team, and the differing viewpoints contribute to the overall effectiveness of manufacturers. The synergy involved improves decision-making and helps the team reach goals within limited time frames.

Efficiency

Teams are able to move faster and more effectively than individual organizations acting alone. This is because they make the most of each member's strengths and talents. In areas where some companies are weak, others are strong…and their combined efforts work together to help manufacturers solve problems.

The best part about the efficiency of a team is that it gets better as the team bonds. Over time, members learn the strengths of others in the group and utilize those strengths when they are needed.

Flexibility

Different organizational "personalities" on a team help the team accept change. Some companies find change challenging or stressful, while others embrace it. This is because people react differently to the same situations based on their perceptions, and those perceptions give teams the flexibility needed to accept change. This is important because change occurs frequently in manufacturing environments.

Idea generation

Companies have different experiences that add to the way their employees think about situations. Team members' individual thoughts generate unique ideas that can be bounced off the rest of the group for problem-solving. This process generates the best ideas because they are evaluated by everyone before being implemented as solutions. This improves the overall innovation of manufacturers.

Divided responsibilities

Teams divide responsibilities between group members, and this prevents individual organizations from being overloaded with work. It also allows members to support each other through cooperation and mutual understanding. In short, dividing responsibilities alleviates the stress associated with being completely responsible for a project...and this relieves the manufacturer of bearing the sole responsibility for improvement.

Risk

This advantage stems from the fact that risk is reduced when SCM is utilized. Supply chain processes and procedures help identify risk factors and determine their potential for harm. This allows manufacturers time to react and make the changes necessary to steer away from possible liabilities before they have a major impact. In short, SCM minimizes risk exposure and allows for effective management of it.

As you can see, there are many advantages to supply chain management. It works well for manufacturers, and this is why the concept is becoming more and more popular. In fact, entire majors in college are based on supply chain management so students can enter the work world armed with knowledge about the subject. However, nothing is perfect. There are some disadvantages to the SCM, and these are discussed in the next section.

Disadvantages

As with virtually every aspect of business, supply chain management has some drawbacks. Below are some of the challenges involved for manufacturers:

Complexity

This is likely the biggest disadvantage of SCM. Many different people and organizations are working toward common goals to make manufacturers more competitive, and this creates a wealth of opportunities for mistakes and problems. Supply chain management has great value for manufacturers, but the problems that result from the components that make up the chain offset some of that value.

Time

The Rolling Stones sang a song about time being on their side. Unfortunately, this is not always the case for SCM. Manufacturers invest massive amounts of time into managing the supply chain. They have to make sure their suppliers are performing at expected levels by measuring important variables such as quality and cost. A balancing act is required because quality must remain high while cost is minimalized. Every partner on the chain needs to be assessed, and this takes time. If SCM was eliminated and the entire manufacturing process was internal, a lot less time would be required.

Trust

Trust is a goal of SCM, but it is a goal that is not easily achievable. In fact, trust can lead to the complete breakdown of supply chain management systems. This is especially true for global manufacturers.

One important aspect of trust involves manufacturers' relationships with their suppliers. They need to believe their suppliers will perform as expected because deviations from expectations are expensive. In short, manufacturers are at the mercy of their suppliers, and this is bad if those suppliers have issues or are unreliable.

Foreign laws

Theft is an unfortunate reality for organizations that operate internationally. The global marketplace is very attractive, but laws in the United States do not protect manufacturers from being taken advantage of in other nations. Loss of intellectual property is the biggest concern in foreign markets. Protection for patents and trademarks might not exist, and this can cost manufacturers millions of dollars in research, attorney fees, and lost market share. One might think that this threat would deter many manufacturers from competing globally, but this is typically not the case. Apparently, the risk is well worth the reward in the minds of the decision-makers.

Uncertainty

Similar to foreign laws, other factors present challenges to manufacturers that utilize SCM in the global marketplace. Please consider the following:

- Nature can create a wealth of problems. Areas susceptible to earthquakes, tsunamis, and volcanic eruptions can lead to disastrous situations that nobody predicted. The entire infrastructure of a nation can be destroyed along with the manufacturer's supply chain.
- Political climate is a threat because new administrations can completely change the rules upheld by their predecessors. If this happens, current ways of doing business are no longer valid...and neither is the supply chain of the manufacturer.

- The economy can suddenly become unstable. If this happens, organizations can go out of business. Obviously, the bankruptcy of a partner would hinder the manufacturer's supply chain as a whole.

You can see that the above disadvantages can spell disaster for supply chain management. That being said, there must be methods for improving SCM, and those methods are discussed in the next section.

Improving

Supply chain management has a lot of upside potential, and this is why more and more manufacturers are implementing it as a part of their everyday process. However, regardless of the benefits of SCM, there is always room for improvement...as long as manufacturers are willing to make the effort.

The following are some suggestions for making SCM better:

Involve employees

This might seem like a rather obvious way to improve SCM, but it is often overlooked. Management tends to forget that their own workers are part of the supply chain, choosing instead to focus on other organizations for improvement. Employees work for the most important link in the chain, and their involvement in the process will help strengthen that link. Additionally, their specific jobs might give them insight into valuable ways to improve the chain as a whole...and this is beneficial to everyone in the system.

Improve technology

No manufacturer is 100 percent up to date in terms of technology. Computerized systems automate and simplify many aspects of the supply chain process, but cost limitations often prevent their implementation. However, one investment that is worth the money is radio frequency identification (RFID). Manufacturers that move thousands of items through their faculties need inventorying systems that are more efficient than bar coding. For these organizations, radio frequency identification (RFID) is the answer. Essentially, RFID uses radio waves to collect information on products and raw materials. That information gathered is similar to that collected by bar code scanners, but it can be read from several feet away. Large numbers of raw materials or finished products can be scanned without the necessity of hand-held units, and these scanners do not have to have a direct line of sight to register information.

Encourage innovation

Manufacturers have a wealth of innovative capacity at their fingertips...if they choose to tap into the talents of the organizations within the chain. These companies have expertise in specific areas that can be used to simplify production and get products to market faster and more affectivity. In short, manufacturers can improve SCM by leveraging the innovative skills of other chain members.

Utilize information

Similar to innovation, manufacturers have a lot of information available from the supply chain that they do not utilize. Detailed data analysis gives them the ability to effectively manage their supply chains from start to finish. Communication with suppliers opens the door to information that can be used to determine customer needs, increase competitiveness, and improve supply chain performance. This information can also be used to develop standards. Manufacturers must avoid the "do your best" mentality because this reduces accountability. Standards give suppliers goals and direction for continuous improvement...and this betters SCM as a whole. In short, information is readily available if manufacturers decide to use it.

Review performance

Performance reviews of organizations in the supply chain can be a very time-consuming process...and that is why some manufacturers avoid it. However, if performance is not reviewed, then weak links cannot be identified and the right partners will not be put in place. Manufacturers need to invest time and effort into the continuous review of companies in the chain so they do not end up in difficult situations that are challenging to resolve. In short, a plan needs to be in place to measure performance, implement improvement strategies, and make the changes necessary to make the chain better. In terms of performance reviews, "those who fail to plan, plan to fail."

Analyze returns

Virtually every organization that manufactures products can expect to get some of those products returned by customers. Unfortunately, many returns are the result of faulty quality...something that should have been addressed in the supply chain. Manufacturers need to spend time analyzing their returns to see exactly where the problems stem from so they can address them in the chain. However, this is typically not the case. Most manufacturers assume there will be a certain percentage of returns, so they ignore them when they come back to their facility. This is a wasted opportunity because, if given the proper attention, returns can improve the supply chain by pinpointing areas where changes need to be made.

Summary

Supply chain management is being embraced by many manufacturers today. It is especially valuable for those who compete globally because it involves an international chain of organizations that work together to produce the best products at the lowest cost. This gives manufacturers a competitive edge in a world where profit margins are lean and competition is fierce.

This book focuses on supply chain management in manufacturing. First, it examines phases of this system and the factors that affect it, next it explores goals and objectives established by management, then it analyzes advantages and disadvantages in the chain, and last it suggests ways to improve the overall process. The text is informational and educational, and it is written for easy understanding at all reader levels.

Congratulations! You now understand more about supply chain management...an increasingly popular concept for manufacturers worldwide.

Inventory Control in Manufacturing
A Basic Introduction

Louis Bevoc

Published by
NutriNiche System LLC

Louis Bevoc books...simple explanations of complex subjects

Introduction — 21
What is it? — 21
Why is it needed? — 21
Why doesn't it always work? — 21

Goals — 23
Track finished products — 24
Track raw materials — 24
Track trends — 24
Prevent theft — 25
Prevent overages — 25
Prevent shortages — 25

Methods — 26
Manual — 26
Bar Code — 27
Radio Frequency Identification (RFID) — 27

Reordering systems — 28
Visual — 28
Fixed time — 28
Fixed quantity — 28
JIT — 29
Safety — 29
Vendor controlled — 29
Collective — 30

Management — 30
Designating employees — 31
Soliciting suppliers — 31
Selecting methodology — 31
Determining reordering — 31
Monitoring inventory for trends — 31

Improving — 32
Maintain inventory records — 32
Generate inventory reports — 32
Implement mobile devices — 32
Increase inventory frequency — 32

Summary

Introduction

Most organizations need some type of inventory control. Companies that manufacture products usually have more physical items to keep track of than those that provide services, but both types of organizations have inventory that needs to be monitored. For example, a marketing company that promotes other companies' products does not have to physically inventory any of those products or the raw materials used to manufacture them. However, that marketing company needs office supplies and materials for sales presentations, and stocking these items requires some type of inventory control.

A complete definition of inventory control can become quite detailed because it depends on the specific needs of individual organizations. However, for simplification purposes, inventory control for this book is defined as:

Lowest cost management of the materials required to meet organizational demands.

This book examines inventory control in manufacturing based on the above definition. Specifically, it discusses important goals of inventory control, methods for performing inventory control tasks, systems for reordering stock, management responsibilities, and ways of improving inventory control programs. The text is informational and educational, and it is written for easy reader understanding at any level.

Now that you understand the scope of this book, we can move into the major areas of discussion. Let's start by answering the following questions regarding the general concept of inventory control in manufacturing:

What is it?

Inventory control is a system that accounts for all items (raw materials and finished products) in stock at a manufacturer. It determines the location and quantity of these items so employees know what is on hand and where to get it.

Why is it needed?

Inventory control is needed for a variety of reasons, but the major ones are as follows:

- It ensures finished product stock is maintained at a sufficient level. Too much inventory results in unnecessary cost and too little inventory results in unfulfilled customer orders. Inventory is expensive, but so are lost customer sales...so there needs to be a balance.
- It can be used to track raw materials or finished product usage. When an item goes out of stock, people who order it are notified so they can replenish supply.
- It establishes reorder levels for raw materials and finished products. Reorder warnings are issued when inventory dips below designated levels.
- It detects theft, damage, and other losses. If inventory is missing but nothing was sold or produced, then there is a problem.

Why doesn't it always work?

Inventory control programs need to function efficiently to benefit the organizations that implement them. However, they do not always work properly for the following reasons:

Lack of planning

It is not uncommon for manufacturers to spend large amounts of money on inventory control software only to find that it does not meet their expectations. This happens for the following reasons:

- Management does plan for operating the system once it is live. They assume the software will run itself because they have invested a lot of money into it. The software will work, but management needs to understand what is needed to make it perform properly.
- Management does not plan for putting the right people in charge of the system. They assume employees will "fill in as needed" and take responsibility for aspects of the program that apply to their jobs.
- Management does not plan for a complete switch over to the new program. Some employees refuse to let go of old inventory control methods unless they are forced to do so. They do not trust or like the new software, so they keep doing things the way they have been doing them….and never learn the new program. Cut-off dates need to be set in advance and enforced.

Regardless of the reason, planning is essential for getting inventory control systems to work effectively and produce valid information. In terms of inventory control, there is truth to the old saying, "those who fail to plan, plan to fail."

Lack of physical inventorying

This is probably the biggest reason for the failure of inventory control programs. Think of the old adage, "garbage in" equals "garbage out" because it is very applicable to inventory control. In fact, it is possible that this saying gained popularity among inventory control professionals.

If the people doing physical inventorying do not enter accurate information, the system will not work. For example, assume 1000 boxes of pencils are in stock at a warehouse. However, the person inventorying this item only enters 600 boxes because he missed three pallets that are in a different location of the building.

This error causes a domino effect of other errors that cannot be corrected until the pencils are correctly counted. When customers buy pencils, the inventory is inaccurate…as is the case when new pencils are ordered. Re-order levels are also inaccurate, so too many or too few pencils could be kept on hand. Add this to the fact that inventory costs are wrong, and the end result is a major fiasco…all because inaccurate numbers were entered during physical inventory.

Unfortunately, these inaccuracies can negatively impact the bottom lines of organizations.

Lack of customer understanding

Manufacturers that do not understand the inventory needs of their customers will not have a successful inventory control program. There must be a basic understanding of customer ordering, and this is best done by tracking trends.

For example, a meat processor's inventory control computer program is designated to reorder turkeys when inventory goes down to 500 birds. This assures a two-week supply will always be on hand. However, the program does not know that 80 percent of the turkeys are purchased two weeks before Thanksgiving...and the company runs out of birds at a critical time. Employees are upset with the computer program, but it is not the problem. Management needs to understand customer needs during this holiday and appropriately adjust reordering levels based on those needs.

Manufacturing personnel become upset when inventory programs do not perform as expected. However, often times the program is not at fault...as shown in the example above. The fault, quite simply, stems from the people in charge.

The following is a list of problems that result when manufacturing inventory control programs do not work:

- Products go missing without being noticed. This prevents mistakes and theft from being detected and rectified.
- Product shortages result from inventory trends not being noticed. This results in unhappy customers.
- Product overstocking is not detected. This results in money being unnecessarily spent and tied up.
- Product overstocking makes storage space an issue.
- Time and money are spent trying to resolve inventory problems.
- Shipping and transportation delays result from a lack of accurate information.

Based on the above, it is fairly obvious that inventory control systems need to work properly or there will be consequences. The next section expands on this thinking by discussing the goals and objectives of inventory control systems.

Goals

All programs utilized by organizations have specific goals or they would not have been implemented. The basic goals of manufacturing inventory control programs are understood by most employees, but that understanding is usually limited to the aspects that affect their specific jobs. The following is a more complete breakdown of inventory control goals for a better understanding of the need for these types of programs in manufacturing:

Track finished products

This is the most commonly known and understood goal of inventory control. Finished products need to be stored and accounted for to meet customer demand. Inventory control programs track the quantity and types of finished products in stock so manufacturers can be confident that they have enough to fulfill orders.

Believe it or not, many manufacturers are unaware of their finished product inventory. They have disorganized warehouses where products are not kept in common bays or designated areas. They also do a poor job of physical inventorying, so quantities being entered are wrong making every calculation that follows inaccurate. Add the fact that these companies have even less knowledge of their finished products that are stored offsite, and it is relatively easy to see why they have difficulty tracking their inventory.

Finished product accuracy is a major reason why manufacturers need inventory control. The complexity, location, and quantity of items produced by some of these companies indicate the need for computerized programs with relevant software. However, manual systems will work if the proper amount of time and effort are put forth. Either way, accurate information on finished products is important for organizational growth and survival, and that is why trend tracking is a major goal of inventory control programs.

Track raw materials

Manufacturers need raw materials to produce finished products. These raw materials are used at various points of the production process, so they must be kept on hand and stored in the facility.

The inventorying of raw materials is similar to that of finished products, except for the fact that the customer is the company itself. Raw materials are only used internally to build finished products, so one department "sells" or transfers them to another during the production process.

Quantities, location, and usage of all raw materials need to be tracked for cost and production purposes. This is done using inventory control programs, and that makes tracking raw materials an important goal of those programs.

Track trends

Organizations that turnover raw materials and finished products need inventory control for many different reasons, and competitiveness is one of those reasons. Inventory systems help manufacturers remain competitive because they generate a wealth of beneficial information. Some of that information, such as sales of individual products, is useful for tracking trends.

Unfortunately, many organizations fail to do a good job of tracking trends, and this gives their competition an advantage. In manufacturing, trends are important because they indicate the need for production during specific periods of time. For example, an ice cream manufacturer understands that sales are higher in the summer, so management must schedule production accordingly. However, before that scheduling can be done, some questions need to be answered. How much sugar, cream, cocoa, vanilla, corn syrup, and ice cream base should be kept on hand to make the ice cream? What type of cartons are needed for the ice cream and how many must be stored? How much of each flavor of ice cream should be ready for sale to customers? These questions can be answered with inventory control. Records allow the ice cream maker to look back on summers of previous years to see what raw materials were on hand and what finished products were produced, stored, and shipped. After a few calculations, raw materials can be purchased and production can be scheduled with confidence.

In short, trends help manufacturers meet customer demands while making their production processes efficient and effective. This makes them more competitive and explains why trend tracking is an important goal of inventory control.

Prevent theft

Leaders of organizations do not like to think that their employees would steal from them, but reality shows that some will if opportunities are present. In fact, most inventory theft comes from employees...and manufacturing plants are always under threat for this type of illegal behavior.

In manufacturing facilities, theft is possible in many different areas of production. Products do not have to be finished for people to steal, and that is one reason raw materials are accounted for continuously. Unscrupulous individuals stop at nothing to make money at the expense of others, and manufacturers are preferred targets because they have so many different items in inventory that can be sold for pure profit.

Theft prevention is critical to leaders of organizations, and this makes it a significant goal of inventory control systems. Since workplaces will likely never completely rid themselves of dishonest employees, this goal will likely never disappear or diminish in importance.

Prevent overages

At first glance, raw material and/or finished product overages in manufacturing plants might not seem like a major issue. After all, the material or product will get used...it is just a matter of time. Although this type of thinking might appear reasonable, it is completely wrong because stock overages cost organizations money. In fact, stock overages can cost large companies millions of dollars a year for purchasing and storage of items that are simply not needed. Additionally, space is required that could be utilized much more efficiently.

A major goal of inventory control is to prevent stock overages in order to save manufacturers money. In this respect, inventory control systems minimize costs and help organizations become more economically stable.

Prevent shortages

Raw material or finished product shortages are fairly common problems in manufacturing facilities. People order wrong quantities, order correct quantities at the wrong times, or simply do not order at all because they forgot or were unaware that stock was needed.

A major reason for shortages is uncertainty. Purchasing agents and salespeople are not sure how to forecast product sales, and this causes them to underestimate. In the end, demand exceeds supply...and the end result is unhappy customers because their orders are not filled.

Effective inventory control systems prevent shortages from occurring in manufacturers. They provide information that helps people make calculated decisions about lead times and quantities of orders. This prevents mistakes from happening that hinder production and produce dissatisfied customers.

Stock shortages create headaches for manufacturers, and that is why preventing them is a goal of inventory control programs.

Inventory control systems show what happens to raw materials and finished products. They track raw materials used to manufacture finished products, locations where finished products were delivered, customers who made purchases, and prices paid for transactions. This information can then be used by management to verify that their company is performing effectively and efficiently. In short, inventory control systems ensure accuracy, and this leads to accomplishing the goals designated in this section.

Now that you understand the goals of inventory control, we can move into the next section that discusses methods manufacturers use for conducting inventory.

Methods

Every manufacturer is different, and that difference is apparent in the ways they conduct inventory. Some companies count every item in the building while others choose to exclude some items, some companies do physical inventorying every month whiles others do it quarterly, and some companies have designated inventory control personnel while others rely on departmental employees.

Regardless of the internal differences, there are three basic methods for conducting inventory that all manufacturers follow. These methods are:

Manual

Manual inventory control is by far the most interesting method due to the creativity and variety involved. For example, some people write inventory levels on the back of paycheck stubs or production schedules while others enter the information into computerized systems. Either way, the inventory is manually entered rather than scanned or read, and it is used to track orders and purchases. That information can then be used to determine reorder levels of raw materials and finished products.

Advantages of the manual method are cost and training savings. The pencil and paper method, for example, requires very little investment and does not require employees to be trained on inventory software that can be somewhat complex.

Disadvantages of the manual method include lack of complexity and reliance on human accuracy. Simple input equals simple output...and this means the inventory system is not capable of generating detailed reports that track trends or provide periodic usage levels. Additionally, people make mistakes...and the manual method is held hostage to those mistakes. One wrong entry can lead to a domino effect of errors.

Bar Code

Bar coding is a preferred inventory method for many organizations because it generates accurate and reliable information that benefits personnel in all departments. Virtually all large retailers use bar coding, and major manufacturers are following their lead.

Manufacturers use bar codes for all types of inventory in their facilities. This technology allows for the tracking of raw materials to determine where they came from, where they are, where they are going, and when they need to be re-ordered. It also indicates production scheduling needs for finished products so management personnel can react according.

The advantages of bar coding are error reduction and time savings. Accuracy is not dependent on human entry, and information can be inputted in a fraction of the time required by manual methods.

Disadvantages of bar coding are cost and breakdown. Some systems are very pricey, thereby limiting the manufacturers that have access to them. Additionally, personnel become dependent on scanners...even to the point where they cannot function if those scanners are not working properly. Manual inventory is not an option because they have never done it. In short, inventory comes to a halt when scanners malfunction, are broken, or are not available.

Radio Frequency Identification (RFID)

Manufacturers that move thousands of items through their faculties need inventorying systems that are more efficient than bar coding. For these companies, radio frequency identification (RFID) is the answer. Essentially, RFID uses radio waves to collect information on products and raw materials. That information gathered is similar to that collected by bar code scanners, but it can be read from several feet away. That being said, some readers are mounted on walls or ceilings as they accurately scan all items that pass by them.

The advantages of RFID are volume and readability. Large numbers of raw materials or finished products can be scanned without the necessity of hand-held units, and these scanners do not have to have a direct line of sight to register information.

Disadvantages of RFID involve technical issues and privacy concerns. In terms of technology, there are no concrete regulations in effect, so one company's system might not be able to be read by another. This is especially troubling when the customers of manufacturers are unable to scan the items they are receiving. Additionally, these systems are difficult to program and there is a constant threat of information being intercepted. Based on these disadvantages, some manufacturers are shying away from RFID...at least until the technology gets better and the risk for problems decreases.

Now that you understand the major methods used by manufacturers to conduct inventory, let's move into specific types of inventory control systems.

Reordering systems

Different systems for reordering stock are used within each inventory method listed in the previous section. For example, one manufacturer might choose to inventory their raw materials and finished products using bar coding while another chooses manual methodology. However, both companies replenish their stock using a fixed quantity system. In other words, they reorder when stock goes below established levels....so the reorder point is always the same. Another example is when two manufacturers both choose RFID for their inventory method, but one reorders based on immediate needs such as stock outages while the other reorders based on precautionary measures such as the uncertainty of supply.

The following are different types of reordering systems used regardless of the method chosen to conduct the inventory:

Visual

This system is typically used by small manufacturers that have a good grasp of the raw materials and finished products they have in their facilities. Plant management knows from experience when they need to reorder by simply looking at the supplies they have on hand.

This system works well when competent people, such as owners, are in charge. However, other employees might not be capable of performing at the same level when competent people are not present. In other words, this system is risky.

Fixed time

Fixed time systems base stock reordering on specific time periods rather than quantity. For example, a bakery checks wedding cake inventory at the end of each week and produces the same number of cakes that were sold during that week. If they sell 25 cakes, then they make 25 cakes. The bakery is replenishing supply based on usage over a specific period of time.

This is a rather simple reordering procedure that works well for manufacturers that have consistent sales throughout the year. However, it does not account for slow and busy sales periods. For example, the cake manufacturer needs to take into account that most weddings take place in the warmer months. If they are not careful, they could run out of wedding cakes at the beginning of May and have excessive stock at the end of September.

Fixed quantity

This system is similar to the fixed time system because it has designated reorder points for raw materials and finished products. However, the fixed quantity system is not reliant or dependent upon time frames. Reordering occurs when stock falls below designated minimum quantities.

This system is advantageous because it takes the guesswork out of reordering. Manufacturers do not have to make decisions about how much stock to keep on hand because it is automatically reordered at pre-established levels. However, it also has disadvantages because those pre-determined stock levels might not always reflect actual needs. For example, a utensil manufacturer might automatically reorder raw materials for a stainless steel line of knives even though that line is going to be discontinued. In this case, the stainless steel is not needed…but the system automatically reordered it when it hit a designated level.

Just-in-time (JIT)

The goal of this system is to reduce inventory holding costs and expose raw materials and finished products that are not used or no longer needed by manufacturers. Stock is brought in "as needed," thereby increasing inventory turnover while decreasing expenditures. JIT is very attractive to manufacturers, and it has recently become a favorite for reordering stock and supplies.

JIT is advantageous because money and space are not tied up in inventory that is not immediately needed, but it is also risky because there is always the threat of running out of stock. "Just-in-time" means stock will arrive at the point of need without anything extra. However, this is potentially hazardous because manufacturers that gamble on stock quantities might not be able to fill orders and meet customers' demands. For example, a door manufacturer might find that certain doorknobs are not available when they are needed…so they are unable to fill a customer's order. This problem causes them to lose the business to a competitor who does not use JIT and has the knobs in stock.

Safety

This system is used when there is an uncertainty of customer demand or the manufacturer has difficulty producing the product. For example, a paint manufacturer makes a bacteria-resistant paint that is currently being promoted by the salespeople. They currently sell 100 gallons per week of this item, but they do not want to run out of stock if customers start buying it, so they produce 1000 gallons for stock.

The safety system works well to prevent products from being out of stock, and it gives manufacturers confidence that they will be able to fulfill orders. However, it is costly due to the cash outlay, and the additional inventory takes up space. Unfortunately, the challenges involved prevent some manufacturers from using this system for their inventory.

Vendor-controlled

Reordering for this system is done by vendors that sell their products to manufacturers. These vendors physically inventory their own items at the manufacturers' facilities and reorder when stock gets low. They are the manufacturers' inventory control, and they assume all responsibility for stock.

This system is advantageous for manufacturers because they do not have to use their own people to inventory and make reordering decisions. However, the other side of the coin is that manufacturers lose control of reordering, and this means money and space can be tied up based on vendors' decisions. Understandably, most vendors will not run out of their own products...but some tend to overstock.

Collective

Some manufacturers use a combination of systems to reorder raw materials and finished products. This is called a collective system where inventory is classified into groups, and each group is given a level of reordering.

This system works well for maintaining proper inventory levels at companies that make a wide variety of items that are costly, consistent in sales, and difficult to produce. However, the downside is that it can be rather complicated leading to errors that cause problems for the manufacturer and its customers. For example, a pet food manufacturer classifies canned dog food (finished product) in one category, bagged dog food (finished product) in another, and lecithin (raw material) used to make both in a third category. The canned dog food uses a JIT system because it is very expensive to manufacture, the bagged dog food uses a fixed time system because sales are consistent every week, and the lecithin uses a safety system because it can be hard to obtain.

Now that you understand the various ways that raw materials and finished products are reordered, let's move on to basic management responsibilities for inventory control programs.

Management

Virtually everything in business is a gamble. Manufacturers gamble that their vendors will supply them with raw materials, their employees will produce quality products, and their customers will pay for items purchased. These gambles are worth the risk, but the same cannot be said for choosing not to implement effective inventory control programs...and those programs will only be effective if they are properly managed.

The process of inventory control can be quite detailed and demanding. Larger manufacturers have entire departments devoted to this specific task, and a lot of time and money are spent making sure the information collected is reliable and accurate. That being said, it is relatively easy to understand why the management of inventory control is important.

The oversight of inventory control programs might appear to be a fairly simple process...but this is rarely, if ever, the case. Management involvement is required before, during, and after the systems are implemented because work needs to be done and decisions need to be made.

The following are specific management responsibilities regarding inventory control:

Designating employees

This must be done before the inventory control program is implemented. If employees are going to do the inventorying, then responsibility needs to be assigned. Will a new department be established or will existing employees take on the routine tasks involved? When should the inventory be conducted? What information needs to be entered? What reports need to be generated? Who gets the information? Who is in charge of the program? Management needs to designate people for the proper functioning of the program or it will not be beneficial to the manufacturer.

Soliciting suppliers

This must be done before the inventory control program is implemented. If suppliers are going to inventory their own products, they need to be told what to do and how to do it. Which products need to be inventoried? How often should inventory be conducted? Does the inventorying need to be done on a specific day or at a specific time? Who gets the inventory information? Who makes reordering decisions? The entire procedure needs to be communicated to vendors by management or the program risks failure.

Selecting methodology

This must be done before the inventory control program is implemented. Which method or methods will be utilized? If a manual method is chosen, then how will the information be documented? If bar coding or RFID are chosen, then what information is needed? What reports need to be generated? What type of computer hardware and software is necessary? Management needs to answer these questions to avoid confusion and unnecessary expenditures.

Determining reordering

This must be managed while the inventory control program is running. Which type of system will be used? Can multiple systems be combined? Are there items that must be stocked at all times? Is floor space a major issue? Is money a major issue? Only management can answer these questions, and the degree of their involvement will influence the success of the program.

Monitoring inventory trends

This must be managed after an inventory control program produces information. Trends need to be continually searched for if manufacturers want to become more effective and efficient. Managers need to pinpoint areas of their business that are growing in sales so they do not short themselves raw materials and their customers' finished products. Along the same lines, they need to find areas that are declining in sales so they do not accumulate excessive raw material or finished product inventories. Trends help manufacturers become more effective and competitive...and managers are responsible for spotting them.

Now you understand some of the major responsibilities managers have in terms of inventory control. The next section expands upon this discussion by examining the ways managers can improve inventory control programs.

Improving

Raw material and finished product inventories are major assets for most manufacturers. Unfortunately, these inventories can become liabilities if they are not managed properly. That being said, inventory control programs need to be improved, and this can be accomplished by adhering to the following:

Maintain inventory records

Inventory records present problems because they are often out-of-date, inaccurate, or unavailable to the people who need them. Accurate and up-to-date records are extremely valuable for improving inventory control programs because they provide a snapshot of products that are sold, products that are in stock, products that need to be stocked, and raw materials that are needed for manufacturing. This eliminates the guesswork and time required to pinpoint organizational needs, and it improves the effectiveness of the overall inventory system.

In short, records provide information, and that information can be used to enhance the value of inventory control programs.

Generate inventory reports

Inventory control software programs are capable of generating many reports that are beneficial to manufacturing facilities. However, most managers are not fully aware of these capabilities, thereby limiting the reports they review to a select few.

Reports help managers identify trends that lead to more efficient operations. For example, they can view stock requisitions, stock returns, stock transfers, stock quantities, order picking issues, and inventory adjustments. If management takes the time to discover what they could have in terms of reporting, inventory control programs will be vastly improved.

Implement mobile devices

Technology is now capable of putting real-time inventory data on hand-held mobile devices. This allows select employees to have immediate access to important inventory information, and it lets them make faster and more accurate decisions that lead to higher customer satisfaction.

Without a doubt, mobile data is beneficial for inventory management. Add this to the fact that most people in the workforce today are fairly comfortable with hand-held technology, and mobile devices make good sense for improving inventory control programs. The only downside to this type of technology is the fact that the upfront cost makes it somewhat prohibitive.

Increase inventory frequency

This is by far the most painful method of improvement. Most people do not enjoy doing physical inventory, but it is a necessary evil of running a successful manufacturing plant. Monthly inventories, rather than year-end, provide a much clearer picture of the stock on hand and what can be done to reduce the cost associated with that stock.

Increased frequency improves the quality of inventory control programs by identifying unused, obsolete, and unnecessary stock that has no value, takes up space, and interferes with productivity. This stock can then be eliminated, reprocessed, or discounted and sold. Increased frequency is especially critical for manufacturers such as food plants that have perishable items in stock at all times.

Increased frequency also helps management identify trends more quickly in order to build upon them or take corrective action. For example, a trend might show that a supplier consistently delivers lower quantities of raw materials than were ordered. This indicates that the supplier is unreliable and might need to be put on probation or eliminated. Another example involves slow-moving items. Frequent inventories bring slow movers to the forefront where they can be dealt with accordingly by trying to increase sales or eliminating them.

Summary

Inventory control is important for all organizations, but it is critical for manufacturers based and the money and space they have tied up in raw materials and finished products. Without effective inventory control programs, manufacturers have difficulty stocking the items necessary to make their products. When this happens, orders are not filled and customers are not happy.

This book focuses on inventory control from a manufacturing perspective. First, it defines inventory control and lists the major goals of inventory control programs. Next, it explores the methods available for performing inventory control tasks and explains the systems used for reordering raw materials and finished products. Then it discusses management responsibilities and examines ways that inventory control programs can be improved.

Congratulations! You now understand more about inventory control...an essential program for all manufacturers.

Human Resource Management
A Basic Introduction

Louis Bevoc

Published by
NutriNiche System LLC

Louis Bevoc books...simple explanations of complex subjects

Introduction — 36
- Recruitment — 36
- Planning — 37
- Compensation — 37
- Training — 37
- Evaluation — 38
- Legalities — 38

Goals — 39
- Compliance — 39
- Commitment — 40
- Classification — 40
- Teamwork — 41
- Diversity and Ethics — 41
- Improvement — 41

HRIS — 42
- Recruiting — 42
- Administering and self-governing — 43
- Scheduling, tracking, and reporting — 43
- Expense — 43
- Security — 43

Disadvantages — 44
- Security — 44
- Mistakes — 44
- Objectivity — 45
- Technology — 45

Future — 45
- Temporary employees — 45
- Remote employees — 47
- Diverse employees — 48
- Specialized employees — 48
- Cost — 48

Summary — 49

Introduction

Human resource management (also known as HRM) was first visualized when managers begin to realize the significance of people in organizations. Employees, not equipment or machinery, were the most important aspect of workplaces, and their efforts were directly related to the success of the business. Frederick Winslow Taylor expanded upon this thinking early in the 20th century, thereby popularizing the concept of workforce productivity. Human resources (also known as HR) departments followed as a means of developing and managing workforce productivity, and that is how the field of HRM came into being.

Today, HRM involves the management of human resources to help organizations meet established goals and objectives. HR personnel find people for jobs, educate them through training, provide them with relevant policies and procedures, and evaluate their performance.

The above paragraph is a rather broad description, and it needs to be expanded upon for better understanding. More specifically, HR people oversee and are involved with the following:

Recruitment

This is likely the most well-known area of HRM because most people associate HR departments with the hiring process. HR personnel select candidates, interview them, and make decisions about whether or not they are a good fit for the organization. This might seem like a relatively simple process, but there is actually a lot of work that goes on before, during, and after the interview. This work consists of:

Specification

Every job that needs to be filled must have some type of pre-determined specifications. This requires the job to be analyzed in order to establish the skills, education, experience, and personality required for the best job fit. This is especially important for newly developed jobs because there is no information available. However, specifications on existing positions should also be reviewed for outdated information.

Strategy

This refers to the strategy used to promote job openings. Who is the job geared toward? Will the job be open to internal candidates only or can anyone apply? Will websites, social media, trade magazines, newspapers, and/or outside agencies be utilized to promote the opening? Answers to these questions provide a method by which potential candidates can be viewed for potential interviews.

Selection

This refers to the ways that the candidate pool is reduced during the interview process. Questions in the interview are designed to uncover information that might not show on a resume. Leadership and interpersonal abilities are brought to light, and specific personality testing is sometimes utilized.

Interestingly, many HR departments take the personality aspect of job fit very seriously because people's traits have been found to predict their behavior at work. Testing is utilized to determine how individuals work alone, work in teams, and work in specific environments. In other words, it shows how potential employees will fit into the culture of the organization. While personality testing is not completely reliable, it does provide insight into the selection process that cannot be obtained by reading resumes or interviewing candidates.

Planning

HR personnel are involved in the planning aspects of organizations, thereby ensuring that the goals and objectives of the company are achievable. This involves employees' identification with their workplace, and it is important because employees who identify with their organization are more committed to its goals. For example, a vegetarian who supports animal welfare probably does not identify with the goals of a pig slaughterhouse. However, that same individual would likely identify with the objectives of an animal shelter for abused pets. In short, there needs to be a plan to make sure the people are committed to the organization that employs them.

Planning also involves understanding employee behavior in the workplace. For example, turnover should be analyzed for patterns that might exist. This information can be used to find causes of absenteeism and low morale that were previously unknown. In short, risk factors need to be identified so they can be eliminated or minimized. This provides leadership with the confidence that their organizations will operate more efficiently over time.

Compensation

This refers to the compensation employees receive for the work they perform. Pay, benefits, vacations, personal days, sick days, and retirement all fall into this category. HR personnel typically do not determine employees' compensation, but they are a critical part of the process because they assure compensation decisions made by management are accurately implemented.

Training

Training is a process where information is provided for educational purposes. Employees acquire knowledge and skills that can be used for enhancing their job performance. They get better at their jobs, thereby becoming more efficient and effective. Additionally, training leads to employees requiring less direct supervision. They are able to do their work with minimal guidance due to the autonomy that training instills. This means supervisors can focus on other aspects of their jobs without the threat of employee mistakes being made due to misunderstanding or lack of knowledge.

One benefit of training that largely goes unnoticed involves psychology. Training improves attitudes and increases morale because employees feel empowered due to the attention paid to them. They realize that they are more than just a "face in the crowd," and their jobs have an impact on the well-being of the organization. Attention also works well for increasing employee commitment. They feel an active part of the organization, and this makes them more committed to its goals and objectives.

In short, many benefits stem from an educated workforce. Employees grow and progress as they become more independent. This benefits supervisors and their organizations. Anyone who has taken on a new work project that is confusing understands the importance of training, and HR people are always at the center of it.

Evaluation

All employees are evaluated by people in higher positions. Sometimes that evaluation is informal, such as an evaluation by an owner of a small company. Other times it is a documented formality that occurs regularly. Either way, evaluations are a method of determining the worth of employees to their organizations. Promotions, demotions, and terminations are often based on them, and wages are adjusted accordingly.

HR personnel are usually an active part of the evaluation process. They might have a supervisor present at the review, but they make sure a structured format is followed to address important aspects of the employee's performance. This format ensures that an employee is meeting expectations in a timely and effective manner. If expectations are being met, then the review can be rather brief. However, if expectations are not being met, then the review can last substantially longer and include an improvement plan that details specific requirements and time frames for completion.

HR monitors the process of improvement plans to assure employees are doing what is expected of them. This process might appear to be derogatory because people's shortcomings come to the surface and are dwelled upon…but that is simply not always the case. In fact, improvement plans can be very constructive, and their benefits include the following:

- They help employees achieve goals that they were unable to accomplish alone.
- They document success that builds employee confidence.
- They help employees realize that they have more to contribute to the organization.
- They allow employees to maintain their jobs while paving the way for future compensation increases.

In short, employee evaluations are important because help organizations accomplish goals and objectives. HR people are responsible for much of this process, and this makes their department a significant part of the organization.

Legalities

This is where high levels of expertise are required because mistakes can be very costly to organizations. HR people uphold policies and procedures, including disciplinary action and terminations, and must understand the legal aspects of situations or they risk the possibility of lawsuits. For example, HR might terminate an employee for stealing based on witness accounts of the situation. However, if there is no video of the actual theft, then it might be hard to prove in court if the employee files a lawsuit. If the company loses the lawsuit, they might have to hire the employee back with retroactive pay in addition to paying attorney fees on both sides. If the company wins the lawsuit, it still has to pay its own attorney fees. In short, it is much better to understand the legalities involved and avoid firing someone without the necessary proof or documentation.

Now you understand some of the major aspects of business that involve HRM. Let's expand upon this discussion by examining the specific goals of HR departments.

Goals

HR departments have a lot of responsibility in organizations. Essentially, they are involved in every aspect of business. Even CEOs have their wages, benefits, bonuses, and other perks monitored by HR personnel. So far, the role of HRM has been described in general. However, there are also specific goals that need to be accomplished including the following:

Compliance

One of the major objectives of HRM is to help organizations avoid legal problems and the fines associated with them. They diligently work to keep companies in compliance with all applicable rules and regulations. As noted in the introduction, this means taking disciplinary action for situations that subject organizations to lawsuit risks. However, it also entails making sure government rules and regulations are followed. For example, there are many OSHA (Occupational Safety and Health Administration) requirements that companies must adhere to or risk the consequences. The United States Department of Labor established OSHA in 1970 with the sole purpose of enforcing laws in industrial and commercial businesses. These laws were created in response to workplace injuries and fatalities that occurred in the US. Companies that do not adhere to the rules can be fined...and those fines can exceed six figures if the findings are severe enough. HRM safety specialists promote safety awareness in workplaces when employees are working around dangerous machines or hazardous chemicals. Their goal is to keep organizations in compliance with OSHA guidelines so workers are safe and lawsuits and fines are avoided.

Along the same lines, HR departments work to comply with all labor and wage laws. There are state and federal laws that apply to minimum wage, overtime, child labor, right to work, family medical leave, and other work-related issues. HR personnel need to understand these laws with the goal of keeping their organization in compliance.

HRM also has a goal of preventing discrimination and harassment. They strive to uphold equal opportunity requirements, promote diversity, and prevent problems from occurring. Accomplishing this goal saves money, but it also has an effect on the perception of organizations. The public does not like it when they read about organizations that allow discrimination or harassment. This activity is illegal, and it results in the company being perceived as unethical.

One last HRM objectively applies to unionized facilities. Grievances related to seniority, overtime, wages, job responsibilities, and other aspects of work need to be addressed…and HR people have a goal of resolving them as quickly and efficiently as possible. They want rules in the contract followed, and they also want to minimize costs to their employer.

Commitment

This is one of the most difficult goals of HR personnel because it is based on individual perception…and every individual is different. HRM wants all employees to be committed to their jobs and their employer. This helps organizations run more efficiently, and it relieves some of the stress experienced by HR people.

To encourage commitment, HR personnel get involved with employees and their supervisors. They work with employees so their voices are heard. Workers who have attention paid to them are more committed to their jobs because they feel like they are an active part of the company. This is supported by the now-famous Hawthorne Studies conducted by Elton Mayo and Fritz Roethlisberger in the 1920s. These studies show that, regardless of the work environment, employees are more productive and engaged when management pays attention to them and involves them in decision-making processes. HR personnel also work with supervisors to improve their communication skills and help them become more empathetic toward employees. Emotional intelligence research started by Daniel Goleman has shown that supervisor empathy is critical for getting employees to become more productive and committed.

In short, the goal of HRM is not just to hire people who are qualified and have the right fit. It is also to get those people involved and make them feel a productive part of the workplace so they become committed to their jobs and their employer. Committed employees tend to remain with their organizations for long periods of time…and longevity fuels the prosperity of organizations.

Classification

This goal involves the classification of job responsibilities and job titles. It is much more important in large companies where employees do not wear a variety of "different hats," but it also has application in some small organizations. Essentially, HR personnel design job titles and related tasks by working closely with management. This leads to clearly defined jobs that neatly fall into place on a hierarchy chart that provides a visual image of the company's authoritative structure.

A hierarchy chart is often a part of conducting business in the United States. Leaders want to know who is in charge of the companies they are working with, and they also want to know who is responsible for making sure their needs are met. Sometimes this process can be rather informal, such as a brief introduction and a handshake, but is never that simple in Asian nations such as Japan. In Japan, a person's title has huge importance, and it should never be disrespected. In fact, it is so serious that the Japanese even place an emphasis on the way their business cards are treated. There are designated places for storing business cards...and a person's wallet or purse is not one of those places. This makes classification one of the biggest goals of HRM in Japan, and that is unlikely to change in the near future.

Teamwork

Teams are important in a wide variety of business aspects today, and that is why many companies are built around a team concept. Teams are able to move faster and more effectively than individuals acting alone. This is because they make the most of individual members' strengths and talents. In areas where some people are weak, others are strong...and their combined efforts work together to solve problems.

However, there are also downsides to teams. Sharing ideas and concepts with others is not always easy. In fact, it can be quite challenging for some people. This is because people differ professionally and personally. Differing opinions, beliefs, and values can lead to conflict...and that conflict is dysfunctional if the attacks turn personal and members focus on position instead of principle.

HR professionals have a goal of making teams the best that they can be. They advise management personnel on best practices for selecting team members and assigning roles. Business priorities and employee skills are taken into consideration, along with an understanding that workers have personal preferences when working with others on group projects. In short, teams are critical for idea generation and problem-solving, and that is why HR personnel have the objective of finding the right fit for members.

Diversity and Ethics

Many organizations, especially those that are global, are made up of employees with a wide variety of backgrounds, skills, and experiences. This diversity is good for improving organizations as a whole, but it can lead to legal and ethical concerns. People with different cultural values, customs, religious beliefs, and social norms can offend each other without even knowing it...especially if the organization is global. Bribery, for example, may be considered unethical in the United States, but it is an accepted practice in some other nations. Along the same lines, derogatory treatment of women in business might be acceptable in certain areas of the globe, but it is illegal in the United States.

HRM has a goal of making organizations diverse while upholding ethical and legal standards. They make sure that employee differences are understood and respected. This is done using awareness programs that include emails, newsletters, manuals, or programs that address culture, spirituality, customs, and social norms of the different groups of people that need to work together to accomplish organizational objectives. Achievement of this goal is critical because it prevents conflict and workplace violence that can potentially be fatal.

Improvement

Like many departments in organizations, HR personnel have a goal of continuous improvement. They want to get better so their company runs more effectively and efficiently. However, unlike other departments in organizations, the improvements made by HR personnel are geared toward bettering every area of the business. For example, the quality control department of a food manufacturer puts an entire day's production of potato chips on hold because they do not meet quality standards. As a consequence, the production department needs to work overtime to remake the product. The action taken by quality control personnel looks good for their department, but it hurts the production aspect of the business. At the same time, the HR department of the food manufacturer announces a training program for improving the active listening skills of supervisors. This program helps all supervisors understand the needs of their employees so the organization can operate more efficiently.

HR personnel attempt to improve all areas of companies including recruitment, training, legalities, ethics, compensation, safety, and healthcare. These areas need to progressively get better for the organization to grow and prosper...and that is why improvement is a goal of HRM.

Now you understand some of the major goals of HRM. That being said, there needs to be a method in place for achieving those goals. That method is HRIS...the next section of discussion in this book.

HRIS

HR functions need to be managed effectively, and that management can be done using Human Resource Information Systems (also known as HRIS). HRIS allows users to view data for HR processes including attendance, payroll, disciplinary action, benefits, bonuses, training, and job classification. It typically consists of a software program that is custom-designed to meet the specific needs of an organization. This program is continually updated as the organization changes, and it is the most important system used by HR personnel.

The following are specific functions of HRIS:

Recruiting

Recruiting is an important aspect of HRM that requires the attention of HR personnel. This makes sense because good recruiting finds employees who can take the organization to the next level. However, if HR people are not careful, they can end up spending their entire day on recruitment issues. This means other aspects of their jobs get ignored...and that is not good for the organization.

With HRIS in place, much of the HR labor that was previously needed for recruiting is freed up for use elsewhere. These systems allow candidates to submit resumes and attachments from anywhere in the world that has internet access. HRIS then searches resumes for key information and classifies candidates based on priorities. This eliminates the work required for resumes received via mail, fax, email, or websites. Classification can be done by education, experience, skills, location...and even public speaking or writing ability. The software handles much of the selection process, and this is a big help for those involved in HRM.

Administering and self-governing

Administration of payroll and benefits is a problem for many HR departments, and HRIS provides a solution by streamlining these processes. Everything is done electronically, thereby eliminating paperwork and providing a permanent record of all transactions conducted.

The best part about this procedure from an HR standpoint is the fact that employees can select benefits, alter tax information, choose retirement plans, and make changes to any of their choices by themselves. They simply log into a website and start entering information that best meets their needs. HR personnel are available for help or consultation, but the time they spend administering information is drastically reduced when compared to the traditional ways of the past.

Scheduling, tracking, and reporting

This is likely the most critical function of HRIS because scheduling, tracking, and reporting are all important aspects of HRM. Examples of this importance include the ability for attendance to be monitored, vacations to be scheduled, injuries to be documented, and data to be analyzed. Additionally, notifications of events, meetings, conferences, deadlines, and other organizational happens can be issued and received by anyone. This allows organizations to pinpoint problems, identify needs, and prepare budgets.

In terms of reporting, HRIS has virtually unlimited capabilities. With a few clicks, reports can be generated that would take hours to research using traditional methods of the past. For example, five years' worth of data on peak periods of absenteeism, turnover rates per department, hours worked for employees, and supervisor bonuses as a percentage of base salary can be collected and put into a report. HRIS produces valuable information in a short amount of time, and this is very beneficial for HRM.

So far, only the positives regarding HRIS have been discussed. Unfortunately, there are also some negatives associated with it. Some disadvantages of HRIS include:

Expense

Cost is a factor for virtually everything in business...and HRIS is no exception. These systems require an initial outlay of cash, and there are also costs for maintenance and updates. Additionally, IT people need to be on staff to oversee the system, and these people can be rather expensive. If cost is a concern, then a cloud-based system might be a better solution for managing HR functions because clouds do not require as much money for implementation or operation.

Security

This is likely the biggest downside of HRIS. Confidential information is stored in these systems, and the release of that information to unauthorized people can create nightmares for organizations. To combat this problem, most companies have different levels of access for employees...depending on their job and rank in the hierarchy. However, no security system is perfect, and sensitive information always has the potential to be leaked.

Now you understand some of the disadvantages of HRIS. However, typically the positives usually outweigh the negatives, and that is why so many organizations utilize this type of system.

Based on what has been written in this book so far, it is rather obvious that HRM is important to organizations because it offers a variety of benefits. However, as might be expected, there is also a downside to employing HR personnel...and some of the negatives are discussed in the next section.

Disadvantages

Unfortunately, HRM is not the "land of milk and honey." It presents some problems in organizations that can fester over time, and if those problems are not addressed they can lead to severe consequences.

The following are some disadvantages associated with HRM:

Security

As noted in the previous section, security is an issue with HRIS systems. Security is also a big concern with HRM as a whole...even if sensitive information is stored on something as simple as an excel file. This is due to the fact that electronic data is vulnerable to viruses that can shut down or even wipe out systems. More importantly, hackers can penetrate systems and do serious damage. Personal information, including social security numbers and bank accounts, can get into the hands of unscrupulous individuals who will stop at nothing to profit at the expense of others. Preventative programs must be in place or there will most likely be some type of breach in security. Unfortunately, many preventative programs prove to not be effective enough to deter illegal activity.

Most of the security issues discussed so far stem from people who are not employed by the organization. However, there are also internal threats from employees. When employees are involved, the system is usually breached for information-gaining purposes, and the action is more unethical than illegal (with the exception of embezzlement). For example, unauthorized employees who access payroll systems can find out what their coworkers are paid and spread that information around the company. This is never good for the organization because it can create jealousy and feelings of inequity because some employees are always paid more than others.

Mistakes

HR employees are capable of making mistakes just like everyone else. However, HR mistakes are often noticed by everyone...such as forgetting to issue bonus checks on the day they were designated to be distributed to employees. There are less noticeable errors such as spelling employee names wrong or entering their tax information incorrectly. While this does not upset the entire workforce, it does negatively impact the affected individuals. Too many mistakes make the HR department appear incompetent or incapable...and this damages the entire concept of HRM.

Objectivity

Objectivity is often lacking in HRM because statistics are the main source of evaluation. Managers often base important employee concerns such as promotions, raises, and bonuses, on numbers rather than looking at the situation objectively. They do not get to know their workers personally and do not see their accomplishments that are not quantifiable. For example, team-oriented employees are willing to let others take credit for accomplishments, while selfish employees only credit themselves. Statistically, selfish employees look better on paper...but this is often not the reality of the situation. Along the same lines, college degrees indicate achievements, but they do not necessarily reflect a commitment to the goals of organizations or the effort put forth in jobs. Non-college educated employees can be better suited for the needs of organizations. In short, statistics paint a good picture of accomplishments, but sometimes they do not tell the entire story.

Technology

HR employees become so reliant on computer systems that they are unable to do their jobs if those systems are not working. This means data is not accessible and the functions of HRM come to a halt. It is also a major headache for employees who want to enter benefit or retirement information when the system is down.

Another problem with technology is the fact that it can be quite complex. Programs might be capable of performing many different functions, but those functions are virtually useless if HR employees do not know how to perform them to access the information. Technology might require outside consultants or training, and both of these are additional expenses.

As you can see, there are some negatives associated with HRM. The combination of these negatives might prevent organizations from hiring HR personnel in the future simply because the rewards do not justify the effort and risk. Supervisors might be told to handle HR-related tasks for their departments or outside services might be contracted to do the work. This leads to the next section that discusses HRM in the future.

Future

Critics of HRM believe it will become obsolete in the future. They argue that software will replace HR personnel, and HR departments will no longer exist. However, there are also people who believe technology will enhance HRM and take it to new levels. When this happens, HR personnel will be added rather than deleted. So, what exactly is the future of HRM? Time will provide a complete answer to this question, but the following will be major factors:

Temporary employees

This refers to contract employees and seasonal employees who work for temporary employment agencies. They work for companies on an "as needed" basis with no guarantee of permanent jobs. These workers are defined as follows:

Seasonal employees

These employees work for specified periods of time (usually 120 days or less), typically during the peak business periods of organizations. They often fill jobs that do not require a high level of skill, but this is not always the case. However, regardless of the skill level, seasonal jobs are critical for obtaining goals established by the organizations that need help.

Many different types of food manufacturers use seasonal employees. Examples include turkey processors at Thanksgiving, ice cream manufacturers in the summer, and candy makers at Christmas. In this role, temporary employees are hired as production workers to help produce enough food products to meet customer demands. These jobs usually do not require a high degree of skill, so employees with a variety of different backgrounds are utilized. In some cases, the people filling these jobs do not even know how to speak English. The jobs are so simple that they can be shown what to do using non-verbal communication. An example includes putting six packaged turkeys into a carton and putting that carton through a tape machine. The employee performs this same process all day long, so specific training is not a factor for the job.

Some organizations require training for all employees...even those that are seasonal. Retailers need seasonal employees during the Christmas season due to the increased shopping demands of their customers, but those employees need some understanding of the company and the jobs they are performing. For example, a clothing store in a mall needs to train associates on how to stock items, assist customers, and operate cash registers. These skills are not natural to everyone, and many people need training. This training is even more critical in the food court area of the same mall. For example, employees who cook food need to be trained on proper finished product temperatures or someone could become ill due to food poisoning.

One last type of seasonal worker is often referred to as a "permanent" seasonal worker. This term appears to contradict itself, but it makes sense because these seasonal workers repeat the same job every year. A lawn care service is an example of an organization that needs this type of temporary help. Lawn care companies call the same people year after year to work for them during the summer months. Fishing vessels also employ the same seasonal workers every year. These individuals are out at sea for a few months, and then they live off the money they earned until the next season.

Contract employees

Contract employees stand out from seasonal employees because they have skills that are needed by organizations. Many of these individuals are temporary employees because they choose to be...not because they cannot find permanent work.

Examples of temporary employees who bring valuable skills to organizations include accountants, lawyers, engineers, scientists, and a broad range of consultants. These individuals contract their services out to companies that need help in specific areas, but do not want to hire permanent employees.

Some contracted employees want to be hired as permanent employees, while others prefer working on a contractual basis. Full-time permanent employees receive health, vacation, holiday, and/o retirement benefits as part of their compensation, but contract employees do not receive any of these perks. However, contract employees have the freedom to control their own destiny, and this is very appealing to some people...especially those who are no longer working out of necessity.

In short, organizations that utilize temporary workers are not responsible for the HR aspects of those workers' employment. The temporary agency that sends the worker out for jobs handles all HR-related aspects of the employment.

In the future, the use of contract and seasonal workers will increase, thereby reducing the workload for HR personnel. This will ultimately impact HRM professionals in companies because their services will not be needed as much as they were in the past.

Remote employees

Employees want to work remotely for work-life balance reasons. Work-life balance involves employees' ability to accomplish work-related goals while enjoying their lives outside of work. This is important because time is limited, and different things need to take priority at different times in life. People need to work to sustain a certain lifestyle...but they also need the time to enjoy that lifestyle.

Telecommuting provides millions of people the opportunity to work from just about anywhere in the world. It helps them find work-life balance and reduce some of the stress in their lives. This is important because excessive stress can lead to fatigue, anxiety, irritability, and deteriorating physical health.

Employees experiencing positive work-life balance are able to step away from their jobs and enjoy life. They worry less, and this helps them go to sleep without thinking about work-related problems. In the morning, they are ready to meet new challenges.

Work-life balance also helps organizations to hire the best Job candidates. If employees work remotely, then they can be hired from all over the world because it does not matter where they live. However, the best people want to be well compensated for their efforts...and work-life balance is an important part of that compensation.

Telecommuting promotes the work-life balance necessary for happy employees, and happy employees are typically less stressed than those who are unhappy. That being said, remote employees will become a larger part of workforces and their HR needs will be handled by internal HR personnel. This means HRM will become more important in companies that promote working remotely.

Diverse employees

In the future, people of all different colors, ages, religions, and backgrounds will work together in organizations all over the world. Teams will benefit the most from this diversity because the combined skills, knowledge, and cultural understanding of members create a synergy that cannot be found in homogeneous teams. Differing viewpoints will contribute to the overall effectiveness and improve decision-making, and this will work well for complex projects that involve innovative thinking.

Diversity will also help employees gain a better understanding of each other's roles in the workplace. Subconscious barriers of cultural judgment and racial intolerance are broken down as employees become more empathetic towards their coworkers.

Organizations high in diversity will rely on HRM for keeping their workplaces effective and efficient. Unique needs will need to be addressed by HR personnel, and this will increase their importance to a level not yet experienced.

Specialized employees

In the past, temporary employees were mostly used for unskilled factory jobs. This has changed, and it will change even more in the future. Temporary agencies will have demands placed on them for employees with specialized skills. Organizations will be looking for temporary help in positions including:

- Architects
- Artists
- Executives
- Human resources personnel
- Researchers
- Trainers
- Translators
- Writers

The progression into more skilled temporary workers will not be difficult because it will come gradually. However, regardless of the speed of implementation, the basic functioning of temporary employment agencies is going to change because they will be taking on more HR functions. In short, the role of specialized employees will increase, thereby reducing the need for internal HRM.

Cost

Probably the biggest factor that will determine the role of HRM in the future will be cost. If it is less expensive to outsource HR functions, then organizations will do so. Add this to the fact that future companies specializing in HR services will be better than they ever were in the past, and it will make sense for many businesses to outsource.

Summary

Organizations today rely on HRM more than they ever have in the past. This is partially due to finding the right people, providing them with policies and procedures, training them if necessary, and evaluating their performance on a regular basis. However, it is also due to the fact the world is becoming a global marketplace...and companies must adapt to compete. They cannot ignore the differences in the people they employ because everyone needs to work together to achieve organizational goals and objectives.

This book focuses on HRM in organizations. It explores the roles of HR personnel, examines departmental goals, discusses the implementation of HRIS, and touches upon the future of this concept. The text is informative and educational, and it is written for easy reader understanding at all levels.

Congratulations! You now understand more about human resource management...a critical aspect of developing and managing workforces.

Customer Service in Organizations
A Basic Introduction

Louis Bevoc

Published by
NutriNiche System LLC

Louis Bevoc books...simple explanations of complex subjects

Introduction	52
Department structure	52
Define goals	52
Establish parameters	53
Hire CSRs	54
Train CSRs	55
Collect feedback	55
Continuously improve	55
Skills	56
Knowledge	56
Patience	56
Clarity	57
Perception	57
Performance	57
Management	58
Closure	58
Reasons for failure	59
Lack of planning	59
Lack of training	60
Lack of consistency	60
Lack of concern	60
Lack of identification	60
Lack of compensation	61
Improving	61
Skill levels	61
Customer incentives	61
CSR incentives	62
Future	62
Social media	62
Technology	62
Self-service	63
Summary	63

Introduction

There is a saying that "you never get a second chance at a first impression." This saying might not apply to every organizational situation, but it certainly applies to customer service. In fact, the person who coined it might have worked as a customer service representative (also known as CSR).

When people talk to customer service professionals, they view them as more than just representatives of the company….they view them as personifying the company. In a sense, the CSRs are thought of on the same level as owners because they are the only source of communication for customers. They answer questions and address concerns, and they speak with absolute authority because nobody else is around to dispute them. Based on this, it is relatively easy to understand that customer service plays an important role in businesses all over the world.

Before going any further, a definition of customer service needs to be established. For this book, customer service is defined as:

> Assistance provided by representatives of organizations for people who have purchased or are considering purchasing those organization's products or services

This definition shows that customer service is critical for sales and marketing. Some people would argue that websites can replace people for customer service. After all, websites can link to virtually anything on the web, and FAQ s (frequently asked questions) can provide information on the most commonly asked questions. Unfortunately, websites simply cannot answer every question or concern, and that is why CSRs are employed by so many organizations. These CSRs, however, are only helpful if they have the right tools and skills to provide customers with solutions.

CSR skills are very important, and that is why they will be discussed in this book. However, those skills will not be developed if the structure of the customer service department is weak or non-existent. That structure must provide CSRs with the right tools to assist customers with their needs….and that is why it is the focus of the next section.

Department structure

There is no "one size fits all" blueprint for the structure of a customer service department. For example, manufacturing CSRs differ from those in retail businesses, and online CSRs have different responsibilities from those serving brick and mortar establishments. Every organization must define its needs for customer service, and then build a department that supplies CSRs with the knowledge and tools required to address customer questions and concerns.

The following is a protocol that can be used for establishing and monitoring a customer service department:

> ### Define goals

Every organization has goals, and those goals need to be factored in when building a customer service department. For example, a company that manufactures computers might have a goal of less than one percent of defective machines. Along the same lines, a retail candy company might have a goal of 100 percent customer satisfaction.....regardless of who is at fault. The point here is that a company needs to define its customer service goals before any other aspects of the departmental protocol can be established.

Establish parameters

Once goals have been defined, parameters to support those goals can be established. This is a critical part of the customer service protocol. Unfortunately, leadership does not always put enough effort into clarifying parameters, and that lack of effort makes it appear as if CSRs are not performing their jobs efficiently. More importantly, it creates a negative perception of the entire organization...and that perception can be difficult to change once customers have it in their minds.

Parameters that need to be established include:

Hours of operation

Will the customer service department be open 24/7 every day of the year, Monday through Friday from 9:00 am to 5:00 pm, or somewhere in between? The hours of operation need to be determined so customers understand when they can get support. This is often determined by the importance of customer service. For example, a credit card company might need CSRs 24/7 due to the potential for fraudulent activity, but a lawn care service might only require representatives to be present during normal business hours.

Protocol

This is important for CSRs so they know how to behave in most situations that they will encounter. Obviously, every scenario that they might face cannot be addressed, but there needs to be a basic protocol in place to establish structure. For example, what questions should CSRs ask to gather information? What should they do when a customer is upset? When do they turn over complaints to higher management? Answers to these questions need to be determined in advance so CSRs are consistent and professional with every customer. It is important to treat customers equally or there could be claims of discrimination that lead to complaints or lawsuits against organizations.

Policies and procedures

Similar to establishing a protocol, this involves the rules CSRs are expected to adhere to when performing their jobs. They need to know their boundaries of authority. For example, what are they authorized to do to satisfy customers? Can they offer refunds, discounts, or coupons? Are there words or phrases that they should avoid saying?

Answers to these questions keep everyone on the same page in terms of policies and procedures.

Channels

These are the methods available for customers to contact CSRs. Social media, telephone, email, website, and live chat are all channels available for use, but they might not all fit the needs of the organization. For example, a dental office might not use social media as a contact, but it likely would be used by a trendy magazine publisher.

The selection of channels should be based on the pros and cons involved. For example, website email (using "contact us" links) is great for describing a situation and sending attachments if necessary. However, email is a slow process that takes time to resolve customer problems. Social media provides a much faster response...but it also increases customer expectations in terms of the time they are willing to wait for that response. Add to this the fact that social media can get very public, and it is easy to see how it is sometimes regarded as a risky channel. Along the same lines, older people largely prefer telephone customer support, but this is in direct contrast with younger generations who prefer computer-mediated communication. Due to these preferences, demographics need to be taken into consideration when selecting channels.

Hire CSRs

Once goals have been established and parameters have been defined, it is time to hire the CSRs. This requires an interview process where candidates are asked questions and placed in scenarios that are likely to occur. Interviewers do this because they are searching for desired traits.

One trait that is critical for CSRs is empathy. They need to be able to place themselves in their customer's shoes to get a better understanding of how those customers feel. Those who are able to do this identify with their customers' needs and provide good service that saves companies money and problems. Poor customer service results in fewer sales which equate to lost money, and it creates other problems because unhappy customers spread ill will to family members and friends.

Another important trait is the ability to communicate. CSRs need to have a complete understanding of the products and services that they support, and they must be able to convey that knowledge so it is understood by customers at all levels. This can be tricky because complex jargon needs to be avoided, but customers also have to believe the CSR is an authority on the subject matter. The key is to prevent misunderstanding that confuses customers and leads them to look elsewhere for products and services.

One last significant trait is diligence. CSRs need to be conscientious and thorough, and this means attention to detail is important. CSRs who rush through the process appear uncaring or preoccupied with other thoughts, and this turns off customers in a bad way. Unfortunately, many customers who feel slighted will never return. Diligent CSRs also tend to stay calm in difficult situations, and this is important because frustrated customers rarely do the same.

In short, CSRs need to be empathetic toward customer needs, communicate effectively, and keep their cool when challenged by irate customers. That is why emotionally intelligent people are often chosen for CSR positions. Emotionally intelligent CSRs make customers happy…and they make companies money.

Train CSRs

Some people might wonder why CSRs require training. After all, their job is to simply answer questions…so study and a bit of research should be all they need. Unfortunately, it is not that simple. In fact, training for CSRs can last for weeks because they must know what to do and how to behave in a variety of different situations. They need to be trained to enhance the traits outlined in the "Hire CSRs" section.

The most important thing about training for CSRs is that it is ongoing. Changes in products, services, markets, management, and other aspects of business require CSRs to obtain new knowledge and information. The most effective and efficient method for learning involves training…especially when multiple CSRs are involved because they can be trained in a group.

Collect feedback

Once CSRs are actively working, it is important to monitor their performance. This is done by gathering information…often times in the form of surveys. These are the type of surveys that many people are asked to take regarding their experience with a representative of an organization. They produce quantitative (number-based) data that provides information about the job performance of CSRs. Quantitative surveys are good because they show how people feel without interference from outsiders…such as someone asking questions during an interview (this produces qualitative data). However, quantitative surveys also lack because they do not allow people to further explain why they feel the way they do about their experience.

Regardless of the method, feedback needs to be obtained to evaluate the performance of CSRs and the entire customer service program. This information can then be used to make changes that make the program better.

Continuously improve

This refers to the changes made to customer service programs after feedback has been received. If customer expectations are not being met, then something needs to change…and it is up to management to make that change. In terms of improvement, customer service programs always need to raise the bar. If they do not continually get better, then they will fall short of meeting the needs of their customers…and competition will be there to fill the void.

Now you understand that a protocol is needed for establishing and monitoring a customer service department. CSRs need to be hired and trained as part of this process, so let's expand upon the hiring and training aspects by discussing specific skills CSRs must have to provide top-notch customer service.

Skills

Many people have experienced poor customer service in one or more of the organizations they have dealt with in the past. This might be due to the fact that the questions they are asking cannot be honestly or accurately answered. Please consider the following as an example:

> A woman asks a CSR at a furniture retailer to recommend a couch that is not going damaged by when her dogs urinate or chew on it. This is a difficult question to answer because the CSR does not know the destructive capabilities of the dogs. If these animals continually chew or urinate on the furniture, then there is no fabric that is durable enough to withstand the abuse. It is hard to make a concrete recommendation for a couch, but that does not necessarily mean the customer will be left frustrated and upset with the furniture retailer. A competent CSR could make the customer feel like she was helped by taking the time to listen to her, showing interest, and suggesting the most durable couch available. This couch has fabric that repels water, thereby limiting urine damage; and it is aluminum framed with no exposed wood for the dogs to chew on. This suggestion does not completely solve the problem, but it gives the customer options and helps her feel like she received some assistance.

Based on the above example, it is rather obvious that certain skills are important for CSRs. The following are specific skills needed for supporting any product or service:

Knowledge

There is an old saying that states "nice guys finish last." This saying might or might not be true, depending on people's individual experiences, but it has never been changed to "knowledgeable guys finish last." This is because knowledge is essential for getting through life...especially in business situations.

Many times knowledge is the single most important skill of CSRs. They can even get away with being a bit rude or overbearing if they have the answers to the questions that customers are asking. Customers want their problems solved, and knowledge often provides the solutions. In terms of customer service, knowledge has the merit necessary to stand on its own...and this cannot be said for some of the other CSR skills mentioned in this section.

Patience

This is the ability to hear what customers are saying without interjecting or becoming emotional. Customers want to tell CSRs about their concerns without interruption, and this means CSRs must know how to listen and exercise self-control.

Listening and self-control are described as follows:

Listening

Listening is the most important aspect of patience. In many ways, it is what a CSR's job revolves around. CSRs who do not listen cannot provide effective customer service. They need to be able to hear and understand what the customer is saying to provide constructive solutions. In other words, they need to actively listen….and active listening often needs to be acquired through practice. In fact, some CSRs find that their active listening skills continually improve over the course of their entire career.

Self-control

This refers to CSRs controlling their reactions. They cannot get mad, sarcastic, or condescending when listening to customer comments. Emotional outbursts need to be harnessed to avoid further upsetting the customer and adding more difficulty to an already challenging situation. This is where CSR emotional intelligence is important because it can prevent an unhappy ending to a conversation.

Clarity

Clarity is an important skill because CSRs need to clearly communicate their responses. Customers who are unsure about CSR intent do not get their questions answered or their concerns resolved…and this can lead to even bigger problems. For example, a CSR tells a customer that he can send back a treadmill that he bought online from Cardwell Manufacturing after he tries it and decide that he does not like it. The customer believes that his money will be completely refunded, but he does not understand that he needs to pay the shipping charge back to Cardwell. When the money is refunded on the customer's credit card, it is $185 short of the amount he paid to cover the return shipping. This infuriates him, and he tells everyone he knows to never buy products from Cardwell Manufacturing. CSR clarity might not have made this customer completely happy, but it would have prevented the situation from turning into a catastrophe.

Perception

This refers to CSRs "reading the minds" of customers. It is an important skill because customers are typically not visible and they do not always say what they mean. When people are not physically present, their body language and facial expressions cannot be interpreted. When they cannot say what they mean, they do not express their concerns or ask the right questions. It is often up to CSRs to perceive the meaning of what customers are saying. For example, an elderly customer calls an electronics store CSR and states that she has been unable to get a remote control she bought for her television to work properly after several different attempts. The CSR needs to perceive the fact that this customer is elderly, and she is not comfortable with technology. Technical support is likely not going to be enough help for her, so the best solution is to offer her a refund.

One problem with perception is the potential for CSRs to interpret wrongly. If they misread a customer, they can confuse the situation rather than clarify it. This causes customers to become dissatisfied…and they might never return. Perception is a skill that requires diligent time and effort to acquire. It is not learned overnight, and CSRs need who fail to understand this are likely to misdiagnose situations.

Performance

In business, most people have to do some sort of acting to complete the tasks associated with their jobs. They play a role in their organization, and that role requires them to move outside of their natural or normal behavior. In the case of CSRs, they might need to be more persuasive than they ever have in the past or they might need to act interested in a situation that they do not find particularly entertaining. Either way, they are required to put on a performance for customers for those customers to feel like they are being properly serviced.

In the words of the famous sociologist Erving Goffman, "we are all actors on life's metaphorical stage." CSRs are actors on the stage of customer service, and their performance often determines their success or failure. Acting is a reality of CSR positions...and this will likely never change.

Management

This refers to the management of priorities and time...not the management of people. Priority management involves organizing tasks in order of importance. Time management involves completing those tasks in a specific frame of time. Not surprisingly, both of these skills are important for CSRs to elevate their job performance.

Priority management and time management are both discussed in more detail below.

Priority management

CSR tasks need to be prioritized because some things are simply more important than others. For example, a heating and cooling company has furnaces go out in two different homes. One customer is at home with two small children, and the other customer is at work. Obviously, the customer with two small children is the first priority...regardless of which customer called first. An astute CSR would recognize this and service the needs accordingly, but a CSR with no concept of priority management might simply service the calls in the order they were received. This example is rather obvious, but the point is that CSRs need to utilize priority management.

Time management

People waiting to speak with CSRs can become very frustrated...and CSRs who do not manage their time properly force customers to wait. CSRs should be friendly with customers, but they should not treat them like friends. In other words, idle chatter and off-subject conversation must be limited so time can be managed effectively. Proper time management by CSRs has a dual positive effect because it satisfies waiting customers and makes bosses happy.

Closure

Customer sales need to be closed in order to be fully successful, and the same can be said for customer service. CSRs need to successfully finish customer conversations, and this can only be done if the customers are satisfied. So, what does this mean? Quite simply, it means that customers feel their concerns have been addressed, their questions have been answered, and/or their problems have been resolved. This is not an easy task, and that is why closure is a skill for CSRs.

One of the worst things that a CSR can do is to end a conversation before a customer's needs are addressed. Sometimes complete satisfaction is not possible, but hard work and effort on the part of the CSR usually produce a customer who is at least partially satisfied. It also prevents problems from building to a point where they can no longer be resolved.

Now you understand some important skills necessary for CSRs. However, those skills are not always applied or effective and, as a consequence, some customer service departments are simply not successful. That being said, it is time to move on to the next section that discusses the reasons customer services departments fail.

Reasons for failure

Unfortunately, all attempts made to establish customer service departments are not successful. These departments fail for a variety of reasons, but the major causes include the following:

Lack of planning

As many leaders of businesses are aware, a lack of planning can cause a multitude of problems. Employees do not do what they need to do, productivity slows, morale is negatively affected, and goals and objectives are not accomplished. Quite simply, "those who fail to plan, plan to fail."

Lack of planning generally results from two major factors. These factors are hiring mistakes and visionary issues, and they are described as follows:

Hiring mistakes

Organizations need to invest time and effort into finding the right fit for customer service positions. These jobs are not meant for everyone, even if those individuals are willing to learn. As discussed earlier in this book, certain personality traits (empathy, communication, diligence) are necessary...and people who lack those traits will probably not be as successful as CSRs.

Visionary issues

Essentially, this refers to picturing what needs to be accomplished by the customer service department. For example, the vision for a company that sells apps for automobiles should be a complete understanding of the app by all customers. However, if management hires CSRs without establishing a clear vision, then the vision is weak and the department risks failure.

Lack of training

In terms of customer service, knowledge truly is power…and training provides CSRs with knowledge. Some companies choose not to train their CSRs in any depth, choosing instead to let them learn by work experience. This choice is a mistake that will cause problems because customers will not be satisfied and CSRs will not like their jobs. Short-term effects will be customers electing not to return, and long-term effects will be the resignation of CSRs. Ultimately, the combination of these effects can result in the failure of customer service departments.

Lack of consistency

People do not want to deal with a customer service department that is "consistently inconsistent" because they never know what to expect. This happens when CSRs establish their own guidelines because (1) guidelines were not provided or (2) guidelines were provided, but they were not enforced. However, regardless of the reason, a lack of consistency means some customers are treated better than others. This favoritism is not good from an organizational or legal standpoint, and it leads to many problems. Customers are left confused, and CSRs become frustrated. Customers begin to look elsewhere for their products and services, and CSRs start to search for other employment. In short, lack of consistency negatively affects the status of customer service departments as they fail to meet customer needs and the goals of management.

Lack of concern

This occurs when CSRs are experiencing personal problems, feel burned out, or simply do not care about their jobs. Personal problems should be left at home, but this is not always the case…as many people are well aware. Burnout is a result of CSRs continually hearing the same customer comments and complaints. Apathy (not caring) is an internal issue that CSRs need to resolve or they should find other employment. Regardless of the reason for the lack of concern, it affects the customers who are conversing with the CSRs. These customers will only take so much of this before they look elsewhere to purchase their products or services…and this means CSRs are not performing. In short, a lack of concern leads to quality issues and can lead to the failure of customer service departments.

Lack of identification

This refers to CSRs identifying with the values and goals of their employers. For example, it would be difficult for right-to-life advocates to work at abortion clinics because they do not identify with the objectives of those organizations. If the right-to-life people were CSRs, they would likely be deterring customers away from the services offered by the clinics. This example is not being used to pass judgment on anyone's beliefs or actions; it is simply showing how lack of identification can cause customer service departments to fail.

CSRs who identify with their organizations also feel empowered. This is important because empowerment leads to people taking ownership of their jobs. When employees take ownership of the work they are performing, they become proactive and accomplish tasks more efficiently. They also require less direct supervision because they self-monitor their performance. In short, a lack of identification prevents CSRs from becoming empowered and this can be the downfall of a customer service department.

Lack of compensation

It is important to recognize the importance of money...regardless of what some individuals might say. An abundance of money does not necessarily make people happy, but a lack of it can make them miserable. This fact is often overlooked by management personnel who believe CSRs should give their best effort regardless of the rewards for their service. Quite simply, CSRs that feel under-compensated will under-perform...and this causes customer service departments to fail.

Some customer service departments are not successful, and the above reasons explain why this happens. However, the problems associated with these reasons can be avoided if companies work at getting better...and that is why the focus of the next section is improving customer service.

Improving

There is room for improvement in every aspect of business, and customer service has a wealth of opportunity in this area. If positive changes are made, a win-win situation is created where customers are happier and CSRs find their jobs more enjoyable.

The following are some suggestions for improving customer service departments and the CSRs within them:

Skill levels

This is likely the most important way to improve customer service, and it can be accomplished through hiring practices and training. Hiring practices need to be improved by putting more time and effort into employing CSRs who are the best fit for the organization. Job requirements need to be defined in advance, and care needs to be taken to make sure those requirements are upheld. This improves the level of quality in customer service departments and prevents a lot of management headaches.

Increased training also improves the quality of customer service. Trained CSRs know how to react in a variety of different situations. They have acquired hard skills, such as technical knowledge about the products and services they support; and they also acquired soft skills, such as listening to what customers are actually telling them. Armed with these skills, they have the ability to answer questions quickly and accurately. This keeps customers happy and prevents sales from declining. In short, educated CSRs are effective...and effective CSRs help organizations reach goals and objectives.

Customer incentives

Unless an organization has a monopoly, it typically has to work hard for sales because people need reasons to become or remain customers. Some of the best reasons involve incentives…and incentives can be improved if CSRs are given the opportunity. Customer service departments improve when CSRs have the authority to offer incentives because customers feel good about the treatment they are receiving. That treatment also establishes customer loyalty, and they speak highly of the organization to their friends and families.

CSR incentives

CSRs are similar to customers in the way that they also respond positively to incentives. Recognition in the form of money, bonuses, prizes, rewards, and paid time off makes them feel good about their jobs. They show their gratitude by going the extra mile to meet organizational goals and objectives. There is a wealth of opportunity for improvement here because management does not always buy into the thinking that CSR incentives create win-win situations. Those in higher positions need to understand that "dangling carrots" provide an excellent return on investment. In terms of management and customer service, one hand truly washes the other.

As shown above, customer service departments can be improved. However, will these improvements be followed through and implemented as time moves forward? That question is the focus of the next section that discusses the future of customer service.

Future

Businesses of the future will need customer service. In fact, customer service will grow in importance because it is the link between organizations and their customers. People demand information about the products and services they are purchasing, and customer service departments provide that information. However, these departments will need to evolve and transform to meet the needs of the next generation of customers. Specifically, these changes will include the following:

Social media

Social media is used by millions of people today, and it is being used in some ways like a customer service gateway. In the future, the use of social media for customer service will dramatically increase because communication is immediate. People will not want to wait for answers to their questions; and Instagram, Twitter, Snap-Chat, Facebook, and other social media will provide the answer. Customer service by social media is a choice today…but it will be a requirement in the future.

Technology

This refers to the technology that is not social media-based. Technological advances are the future of many different aspects of business…including customer service. The software will be commonly used to enter data and track trends. CSRs will be able to produce information in seconds, thereby aiding customers faster and more accurately than ever.

The advent of technology also means that CSRs will be more skilled. Those skills were discussed in the improvement section of this book, and they will continue to expand and become more complex. In short, CSRs will be better educated and financially compensated based on their technological expertise.

Self-service

The world is fast becoming tech-savvy. As younger generations mature, they will not need someone to guide them through every step of web-based or computer-mediated processes. They will understand self-help menus for customer service and will be able to find answers to simple questions. This will reduce some of the demand for CSRs...but it will never eliminate that demand because help will always be needed in some form. Products and services will become more detailed and complex and they will require explanation by qualified CSRs.

Summary

In one way or another, customer service has been around as long as business has been conducted. Over time, it has become quite complex and is now more important than it has ever been in the past. it requires entire departments with skilled representatives who continually strive to improve. Social media and technology have helped shape customer service into its present state, and it will continue to evolve in the future.

This book focuses on customer service in organizations. It examines departmental structure, analyzes representatives' skills, explores reasons for failure, suggests methods of improvement, and discusses the future of the concept. The text is informational and educational, and it is written for easy understanding at all reader levels.

Congratulations! You now understand more about customer service...and an important aspect of every organization.

www.ingramcontent.com/pod-product-compliance
Lightning Source LLC
Chambersburg PA
CBHW070400190526
45169CB00003B/1052